Thomas Wester, as well as being a cat lover, is a
leading Swedish photographer. He has been
photographing cats for twenty years.

THOMAS WESTER

THE
SEASONAL
CAT

Grafton Books

A Division of HarperCollins*Publishers*

GraftonBooks
A Division of HarperCollins*Publishers*
77–85 Fulham Palace Road,
Hammersmith, London W6 8JB

Published by Grafton Books 1991
9 8 7 6 5 4 3 2 1

First published in Great Britain by
Souvenir Press Ltd 1989

Originally published in Sweden by
Trevi Publishers as a calendar under
the title *Katter året Runt*

A CIP catalogue record of this book
is available from the British Library

ISBN 0-586-21058-X

Printed in Great Britain by
Scotprint, Musselburgh.

Set in Palatino

THE SPRING CAT

Stately, kindly, lordly friend
    Condescend
Here to sit by me, and turn
Glorious eyes that smile and burn,
Golden eyes, love's lustrous meed,
On the golden page I read.

All your wondrous wealth of hair,
    Dark and fair,
Silken-shaggy, soft and bright
As the clouds and beams of night,
Pays my reverent hand's caress
Back with friendlier gentleness.

From 'To a Cat'
ALGERNON CHARLES SWINBURNE
(1837–1909)

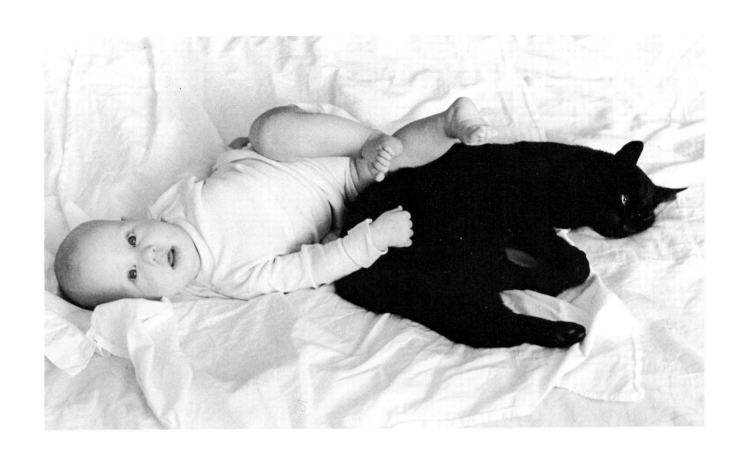

THE SUMMER CAT

Dear creature by the fire a-purr
  Strange idol, eminently bland,
Miraculous puss! As o'er your fur
  I trail a negligible hand . . .

An exquisite enchantment falls
  About the portals of my sense;
Meandering through enormous halls
  I breathe luxurious frankincense.

An ampler air, a warmer June
  Enfold me, and my wondering eye
Salutes a more imperial moon
  Throned in a more resplendent sky

Than ever knew this northern shore.
  Oh, strange! For you are with me too,
And I, who am a cat once more,
  Follow the woman that was you.

From 'The Cat'
GILES LYTTON STRACHEY
(1880–1932)

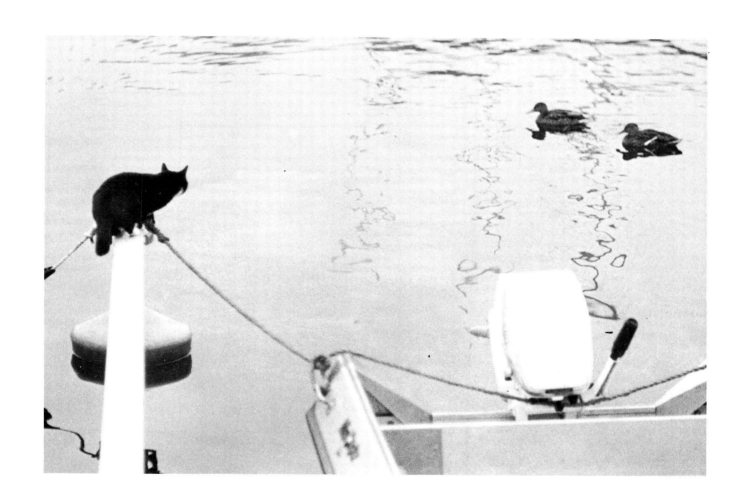

THE AUTUMN CAT

Cat! who hast pass'd thy grand climacteric,
  How many mice and rats hast in thy days
  Destroyed? How many titbits stolen? Gaze
With those bright languid segments green, and prick
Those velvet ears — but pr'ythee do not stick
  Thy latent talons in me — and upraise
  Thy gentle mew — and tell me all thy frays,
Of fish and mice, and rats and tender chick.
Nay, look not down, nor lick thy dainty wrists —
  For all thy wheezy asthma — and for all
Thy tail's tip is nick'd off — and though the fists
  Of many a maid have given thee many a maul,
Still is that fur as soft, as when the lists
  In youth thou enter'dest on glass bottled wall.

'To Mrs Reynolds' Cat'
JOHN KEATS
(1795–1821)

THE WINTER CAT

When the tea is brought at five o'clock,
and all the neat curtains are drawn with care,
The little black cat with bright green eyes
Is suddenly purring there.

At first she pretends, having nothing to do,
She has come in merely to blink by the grate,
But though tea may be late or the milk may be sour,
She is never late . . .

The white saucer like some full moon descends
At last from the cloud of the table above;
She sighs and dreams and thrills and glows,
Transfigured with love . . .

A long dim ecstasy holds her life;
Her world is an infinite shapeless white,
Till her tongue has curled the last holy drop
Then she sinks back into the night,

Draws and dips her body to heap
Her sleepy nerves in the great arm-chair,
Lies defeated and buried deep
Three or four hours unconscious there.

From 'Milk for the Cat'
HAROLD MONRO
(1879–1932)